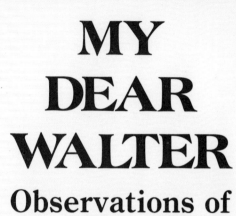

MY DEAR WALTER

Observations of a Gurkha Officer 1937-43

PORTLAND
(R. W. Morland-Hughes)

Foreword by
General Sir John Hackett
GCB CBE DSO MC

Q

Quiller Press
London

THE FLAG STILL FLIES.

First published in 1987 by
Quiller Press Ltd
50 Albemarle Street
London W1X 4BD

ISBN 0 907621 82 1

Designed and produced by Linda Wade
Photography by Delmar Studio, Taunton

Set in Century
by SX Composing Ltd.
Printed in Portugal by Printer Portuguesa

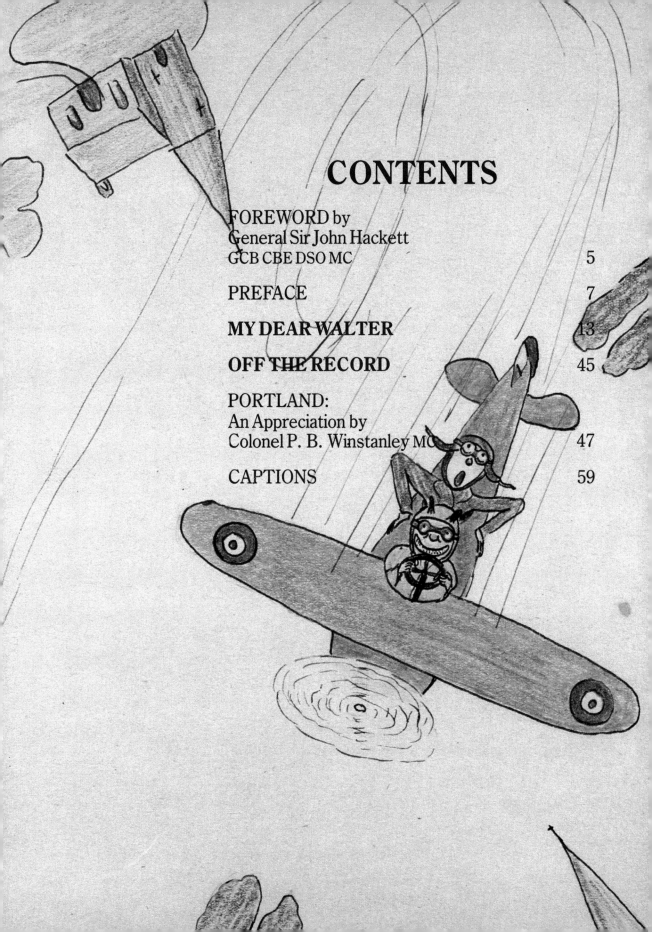

CONTENTS

FOREWORD by
General Sir John Hackett
GCB CBE DSO MC   5

PREFACE   7

MY DEAR WALTER   13

OFF THE RECORD   45

PORTLAND:
An Appreciation by
Colonel P. B. Winstanley MC   47

CAPTIONS   59

WELCOME HOME !

FOREWORD
BY GENERAL SIR JOHN HACKETT
GCB CBE DSO MC

No-one in this country should need reminding of the splendid service rendered to it by soldiers enlisted in a distant, mountainous land, beautiful but harsh and poor, the country known as Nepal, the home of the Gurkhas. As the years go by the tale of service by Gurkha soldiers to the British Crown mounts up. Nearly 170 years have passed since it began – years in which the courage, cheerfulness and loyalty of the Gurkhas have never failed, characteristics which have repeatedly promoted a special, close relationship with their British comrades-in-arms. In two world wars 375,000 Gurkhas served, winning twelve VCs and countless other awards for gallantry, and many others have fought in different parts of the world such as, most recently, the Falklands. Men and women everywhere grow older. Nepal is a poor country, unable to furnish the welfare services these people deserve. There are at present some 450,000 ex-Gurkha soldiers and their dependants who look to the Gurkha Welfare Trusts maintained in Britain to help meet some of their more pressing needs.

It is to provide a contribution to these Trusts that this book is now being published and put on sale. It deserves attention on that account alone. In itself, however, in these letters written by one British Officer serving with Gurkhas to his brother, both now dead, with charming and lively illustrations, it is a delightful memento of a time now moving back into history, the period of the British Raj. Some day justice will be done to British rule in India, when some 45,000 British personnel, civil and military, administered and kept the peace in a sub-continent of teeming millions, marked by almost constant strife since British rule ended. The contribution of the most enlightened colonial system the world has ever seen to the welfare of the hugely varied people of a vast land mass will then be recognised, and the part played in that enterprise, and in warfare almost world wide, by Gurkha soldiery serving the British Crown will find a properly honoured place.

In the meantime this endearing little work will help to throw a lively light on a way of life of high attraction and absorbing interest, which in and for itself should never be forgotten.

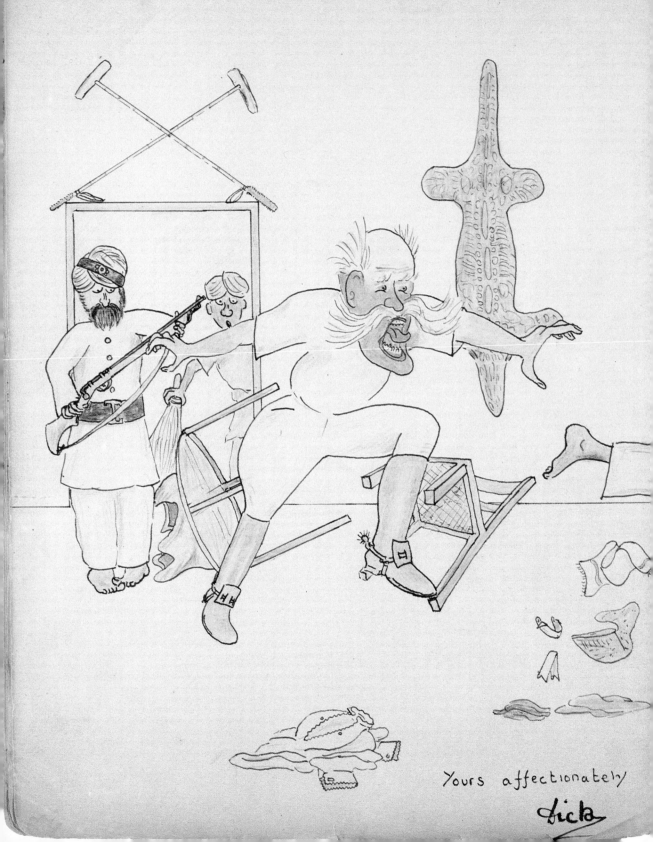

Yours affectionately

dick

PREFACE

It is hoped that the reader will not only be entertained by this little book but will also draw comfort from the knowledge that all profits from its sale will be donated to the Gurkha Welfare Trusts whose purpose is to give some return for the loyal and devoted service the Gurkhas have for so long rendered to the Crown by providing assistance to Gurkha pensioners or their dependants in need. The author, R.W. Morland-Huges ('Dick' to his family, 'Portland' to his Regiment) served with the 5th Royal Gurkha Rifles (Frontier Force) from 1932 until his death in action in 1944. The first part of the book consists of the letters he wrote to his teenage brother, Walter, during his long leave in 1937. They are reproduced here exactly as written, complete with spelling mistakes – one weakness Portland never fully mastered. He had carried on this style of correspondence with Walter for the previous eight years, always writing at a level appropriate to Walter's age.

Through the kindness of Colonel P. B. Winstanley MC, Chairman of the 5th Royal Gurkha Rifles Regimental Association, a summary of Portland's regimental service and an appreciation of his character will be found on page 47. Colonel Winstanley's assistance in making available for publication the collection of Portland's cartoon-style drawings entitled 'Off the Record' – which form the second part of this book – and for providing the explanatory captions which appear on pages 59 and 60, must also be gratefully acknowledged.

A warm tribute is due to General Sir John Hackett. Though he had never served in a Gurkha unit and knew nothing of Portland or his family at first hand, his response when approached for a foreword was characteristically generous. His contribution carries all the more weight through being the views of a highly experienced outside observer. That this book has now seen the light of day is due in no small part to his readiness to be associated with the project and to his helpful advice.

Finally, acknowledgement must be made of the extremely co-operative attitude of the Quiller Press. It is difficult to judge how much appeal a work of this unusual if not unique nature will have but Quiller Press was willing to chance its arm and, once publication was agreed, its guidance has been invaluable.

Richard Wethered Morland-Hughes

Dick (as he was known to his family) was born in London on 25 April 1911, the eldest of five children and the fifth generation of an Army family. In 1914 his paternal grandmother, the widow of an Indian Army Major-General, came to live with the family. After twenty years in India, the tales she told of Army life there kept the children enthralled, and Dick would have learnt from her that his great-great-grandfather had served in Wolfe's army at the siege of Quebec in 1759, and that his great-grandfather, who had seen action in many countries during his forty years as a soldier, had commanded the Regiment in which her own father had served. With her own husband (Dick's grandfather) had come the switch from the British to the Indian Army; her elder son had followed suit, and with her eldest grandson (born in 1897) in the Gurkhas the tradition of military service was maintained. No wonder Dick was set on a military career from an early age.

In 1920 the family moved to Dover, a garrison town of Brigade strength, and there in 1924, when Dick was thirteen, his grandmother died. He followed his father, uncle and first cousins in going to Dover College, which then had the reputation of being an Army-orientated school. He suffered, however, from two handicaps: like his father (who had been unable to go into the Army for medical reasons), he was asthmatic, and, it would seem, dyslexic as well. He refused to give in to his asthma and eventually, helped perhaps by will-power, he outgrew the complaint. His inability to spell was to prove more serious. Dyslexia, if that was the cause, was not then generally recognised, if known at all. At the age of sixteen Dick's spelling was still largely phonetic and his headmaster was of the opinion that because of this he would never pass an examination. Further academic progress blocked, Dick left school with his father's agreement and cast around for suitable employment. It was then that he learnt of Y cadetships – whereby candidates with the right qualifications could enter Sandhurst via the ranks of the Regular Army. Dick saw his opportunity: at seventeen he would be able to join the Territorial Army, and at eighteen the Regular Army.

A natural leader, Dick spent the intervening time creating various diversions for his family and friends (including, among other literary efforts, the *Daily Uproar*, a handwritten newspaper of four quarto pages) and, more responsibly, assisting the general secretary of the local YMCA with fund raising and other activities. He turned seventeen in April 1928 and joined the local branch of the Territorial Army, the 4th Battalion the Buffs (East Kent Regiment) as a private soldier. He spent as much time as he was allowed, over and above the standard quota of

parades, on Battalion duties, including office work and administration, to gain as much experience as possible. More importantly, he had to pass an examination for the Army First Class Certificate of Education, a prerequisite for acceptance as a Y cadet. He enlisted the help of the Garrison education officer and by October 1928 had passed. The following April, aged eighteen, he enlisted as a private soldier in the Regular Army at the Buff's depôt in Canterbury. After his initial training, he was posted to the 2nd Battalion, stationed at Aldershot. As at the depôt, he took part in many official off-duty activities, including membership of the Battalion's rugby, shooting and boxing teams. He was promoted to Lance Corporal and then, judged officer material, to Lance Sergeant (acting, unpaid).

Dick entered the Royal Military College, Sandhurst, in 1930, after eighteen months in the ranks. Once there, he did not relax for, academically, there was still much ground to make up. He had managed to improve his spelling, though it was still unreliable (and remained so to the end). Possibly by way of compensation, he was blessed with a quick and retentive memory. He could reproduce accurately the gist of anything he had heard once, and sometimes word for word. To bring himself up to the highest possible standard, he rose at 4 a.m. daily to study. His diligence was repaid for he passed second out of Sandhurst and, being the senior cadet for the Indian Army, was awarded the Blackwood Sword of Honour. Granted his commission in 1931, he travelled to India where he spent, as was customary, a year on the Unattached List, Indian Army (this year is passed, by way of acclimatisation and language studies, on attachment to a British regiment – in Dick's case the Welch Regiment). This successfully completed, he was assigned in 1932 to the regiment of his choice, the 5th Royal Gurkha Rifles (Frontier Force). This marked the true beginning of his military career, covered in some detail by Colonel Winstanley in his Appreciation which begins on page 47.

Walter Robert James Morland-Hughes

Walter was born on 7 May 1923. Like Portland, he was educated at Dover College where he became head boy. On leaving school in December 1941 he enlisted in the Army and in due course, having been sent to Bangalore as an Officer Cadet, he was granted an Emergency Commission. He was still serving with the 3rd Queen Alexandra's Own Gurkha Rifles when the war ended and whilst on internal security duties during the unrest which followed the partition of India, he contracted poliomyelitis. He died on 7 November 1947, aged twenty-four. He had hoped to obtain a regular commission and be accepted by one of the Gurkha regiments remaining in the service of the Crown. A few days before he fell ill he heard that his appearance before a Regular Commission Board had been successful and that he had been posted to the 10th Princess Mary's Own Gurkha Rifles. In the space of his brief career he managed to compile and have published *A Grammar of the Nepali Language*. His Commanding Officer, who had also been acquainted with Portland, considered that Walter, too, was the type of officer the Army could ill afford to lose. In his CO's words, 'He was most popular with both officers and men ... He was always cheerful, incredibly keen, he had the men's interest very much to heart and nothing was too much trouble for him.'

There can be no doubt that both Portland and Walter would approve of the use to which their letters are now being put.

Explanatory note

Page 26: Cow Lewin (instead of Kowloon) was a friend of the family, 'Cow' being a nickname acquired at school.

Page 27: Portland's verse here is a parody of a rhyme current in Staffordshire after the introduction of willow pattern ware. Slight variations occurred, although the general sense remained unchanged:
Two birds flying high/Chinese vessel sailing by/Weeping willow hanging o'er/Bridge with three men if not four/Chinese temple, there it stands/Like the lord of all the lands/Apple tree with apples on/And there's a fence to end my song.

When Greek meets Greek

MY DEAR WALTER

CIRCUMNAVIGATION

ITS LOVE THAT MAKES THE WORLD GO ROUND.

LANDI KOTAL.
N.W.F.P.
INDIA.
10ᵗʰ APRIL 1937.

My dear Walter,

    I know you will be pleased

to hear that my Colonel Sahib

is a nice man again and that

with any luck I shall be starting

off on leave on the 19ᵗʰ of this month.

Yesterday   Today.

When Greek meets Greek

    I am coming home by Suez and trust

that I shall find that you have done

all that Latin and Greek I hear so much about

when ever I ask for replies to my letters.

    Keep a look out for me at Southampton on 10ᵗʰ May.

Yours affectionately,

THE GREAT INDIAN SOAP TRICK

15th MAY 1937.

MY dear Walter,

Mother and I will visit you at
Dover next Sunday. Mother has not yet
made up her mind about what she will wear,
but I shall put on the old School Tie
for the occasion.

I note all you say about obtaining
the Headmasters permission for you to lunch out
with us. I am not, however, worrying whether
he will let you out, so much as whether he
will let me in.

If you have a young friend who
knows nothing about cars, is not the
son of the Commander-in-Chief,
and will not expect me to help him
light his cigarettes, you can bring
him with you — otherwise forget it.

Yours affectionately

Dick.

A TRIBUTE TO A WIZARD

CANADIAN PACIFIC
R.M.S.
DUTCHESS OF ATHOLL

CABIN CLASS
CONCERT
IN AID OF
SEAMEN'S CHARITIES
Wednesday 15th Sep 1937

TOMMY NIXON OF
TIMMINS N. Ontario.

THE OLD FIRM

Where did that
one
go to ?

will observe, Ladies and Gentlemen, that there is nothing up my sleve except

WINNIPEG,
MANITOBA.
25th Sept 1937.

My dear Walter,

Canada is a swell place — believe me baby! and I am having the time of my life. The following chart is attached in order to show you some of the time I am having.

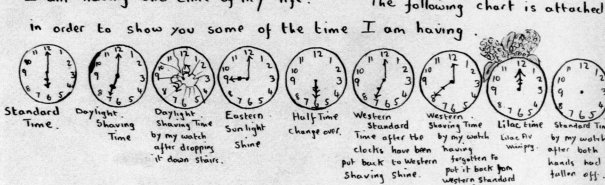

| Standard Time. | Daylight Shaving Time | Daylight Shaving Time by my watch after dropping it down stairs. | Eastern Sun light Shine | Half Time change over. | Western Standard Time after the clocks have been put back to Western Shaving Shine. | Western Shaving Time by my watch having forgotten to put it back from western standard Time. | Lilac time Lilac Av Winipeg. | Standard Time by my watch after both hands had fallen off. |

Apart from "time", Canadian life appears to be normal with the exception of the imported American custom of putting collars round cups.

Other things imported from America include short snappy expressions, long drawn out footballs, Drug Stores and gangplanks. (American!)

At Montreal I was commanded to walk down a gang plank and did so after the arrival of an interpreter.

Yours affectionately

Dick

Take your seats for

Vancouver and the Rockies.

Rocking Horse Pass
Rocky Mountains
B.C.

INDIAN LOVE CALL .

VANCOUVER
2nd Oct 1937 B.C.

My dear Walter,

Take a gander (Canadian) at your

Atlas and you will see that the great provinces
of Catchaskatchean, Al Johnson and B.C. (i.e the
wild west), lie between Winnipeg and the more pacific coast.

(Canadian!)

Before one can get there, however, one has
to pay two cents tax on every meal eaten in

Scratchascatscan.   This is known as

The Great (customs) Barrier and makes the west
wilder than ever.

A good dodge.

All the way through the Rockies
they keep on changing the clocks about
from Daylight Shaving Time to Bed Time
and back again.   This is known officially
as "Mountain Time" and "Pacific Time", but really
it is a clever dodge on the part of the
Railway Company to hide the fact that the
train is running late.

Passing the GREAT DIVIDE the date, as well as the clock, goes back,
for then one is in B.C.   Consequently, the Railway Company does not
give one much time for rubber necking around as they have to get
back to Pacific Time (and A.D.) before the Boat Sails.

Orchids to you (very Canadian),

Dick

HERE FOR GOOD !

Hawaii 7th Oct 1937.

HONOLULU
Hawaiian Islands
8ᵗʰ Oct 1937.

My dear Walter,

I managed to tear myself
away from Waikiki Beach at the
last moment and so caught the ship alright.

Tearing away.

We are now on the high seas for
Japan, but, before we get there, we have to
cross a whole string of dates known as
the Pacific Date line. According to my
Steward, when we cross this line we will go
to sleep on Tuesday and wake up on Thursday.

This seems to be the normal custom of
some people on board ship anyway, so
why worry?

why worry?

I hope most of this terms horrors
will be over by the time you get this
letters. I will tell you all about
Japan when I get there.

Yours affectionately,

The Terms Horrors.

THE RISING OR SETTING SUN?   16th Oct. 1937.

TOKYO
16 OCT 1937.

My dear Walter,

I have just passed the stiffest
medical examination In the world.

This does not mean that you can write 'M.D'
after my name, but that I can walk about
with comparative freedom in ꓵꓲꓤꓲꓤꓳꓠ —
the land of the Cherry Blossom (Kiwi, Meltonia,
Sweedish matches, English Coronation Souveniers, etc.)

Judging from the form one is requested to fill up
(and return to the Purser without delay) one's own ailments
are of little or no inportance. It is the diseases
enjoyed by one's grandparents that score most marks.

"SAY 賈晨同"

The worst thing that can happen to one in Japan is to be caught
with a Camera. The next is to be a Japanese subject.

All cameras are immediately confiscated and exported to Europe.
labled "made in Scotland" and the owner, provided he is not a Japanese subject,
is allowed to leave the country after a few years in jail.

The Chief Japanese industry, after the export of conficated
cameras, is the manufacture of American citizens.

At the moment I am in TOKYO where the Emperor also
lives. After the MIKADO (or town of Tiputoo by Gilbert
and Sulivan) the most IMPORTANT thing in Japan is
the PYJAMA MOUNTAIN. It is believed
that the Gods live in this mountain
and, by some irreverent people, possibly
in the pyjamas too.

THE PYJAMA MOUNTAIN.

Japan is some times called "the Island Empire",
but this is no longer con sidered a good joke in
China and definately bad geography.

But more about China later.

Yours affectionately,
Dick

Bad Geography.

"JAPUNEASY"

My dear Walter,

Here I am again, feeling like John Bull in a China Shop.

I am not sure whether I am at the place I am meant to be as I have not found HONG KONG yet.

JOHN BULL IN A CHINA SHOP.

The place in which I am staying is called Victoria and they tell me that Cow Lewin is on the other side of the Harbour, but I have not seen him yet.

"THE BRITISH SPEAR OF INFLUENCE"

This Colony came under the BRITISH Spear of Influence in 1842 and has not looked back since.

It calls itself a free port in order to attract visitors, but, in practise, one has to pay for everything one has and the only people who get away with it are those who live on the water.

They are called the floating population of HONG KONG and, therefore, do not have to pay anything, so long as they keep on floating.

This is known in Chinese as 大不列顛 BRITANIA which means,

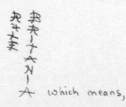
The floating population.

" The FREEDOM OF THE SEAS", but if they put so much as one foot on the bottom they are immediately charged ground rent and may even have to hire a bathing box.

Yours affectionately,

Two planes flying high.

Nippons Warship passing by.

Weeping widdows bending 'ore

battered corpses by the score.

Chinese Pillbox, there it stands,

Till destroyed by Savage hands.

Apple tree with blossom gone.

And here's a bomb to end the song.

CHINA PROPER.

My dear WALTER,

Unlike HONG KONG,
CANTON is not within the British spear
of influence.

It is in China proper and, therefore, ought to
belong to Japan.

I travelled by the Canton
Kowloon Railway from Hong Kong.

TYPICAL CHINESE CITY.

CANTON is much more Chinese
than Hong Kong which is rather pro British.

I am told, however, that even so it is not
really a typical Chinese city.

Probably this is due to the fact that the
Japanese, through some oversight, have left one
or two buildings standing.

The Cantonese looked much the
same as the people of HONG KONG, except
that European clothes were not much in
evidence and the most popular form of
headress seemed to be the "tin hat"

European clothes not much
in evidence.

or, yours affectionately,

Dick

NON EUROPEAN
OR
CHINESE EXTRACTION.

MALACCA
7th Nov 1937.

My dear Walter,

I have just reached Malacca after visiting the State of Johore.

Malaya seems to be a good place for rubber, cocoanuts, bananas and Malays.

Good place for the Malays.

Before the railway reached Singapore.

Malacca was the CLAPHAM JUNCTION of the EAST in 1100 A.D., before the railway had even reached Singapore, but the Portuguese and the Dutch kept on fighting over the place and so, in the intrest of PEACE and the LEAGUE OF NATIONS, Great BRITAIN annexed it in 1794 (i.e. Spear of influence).

The other places I shall visit in Malaya are PORT Swettenham, Kula Lampur and Penang, after that we reach Rangoon which is in Burma.

Yours affectionately,

Dick

Sweating ham.

PENANG
13th Nov 1937.

My dear Walter,

This is good bye to Malaya.

We have cast off from our bouy, weighed the anchor, sounded the hooter and are making for the open sea.   The only remaining act of seamanship is to drop the pilot. This will probably be done round the corner out of sight.

Feats of seamanship.

Mutiny — or the Vulgar Boat Song.

"QUIS SEPARABIT" or "Naval discipline once more" and so, bending on our oars, we sing the Passengers Lament, or Vulgar Boat Song — "Wrap me up in my old safty jacket" — BUT, not so loud that the Captain can hear!

Unlike the crew, mutiny holds out no hopes of redress for the passengers.

The ships Officers hold all the cards.

They can turn on the wireless unexpectedly, at full blast, in the most hushed part of the afternoon, or turn off the bar unexpectedly, at full blast, in the most thirsty part of the night.   They can make the ship go faster and so ruin the daily sweep on its run, stop it suddenly at BATH time, make it vibrate at SHAVING time, or tip it up and down at meal time.

In fact they can make life pretty grim and goodness knows what they can't do with the clocks.

Every thing is all right, however, if you

1) Tie your safty jacket as TIGHT as you can.

2) Place your cigarette end in the box provided. (If it burns your fingers before you find the box, you are allowed to change hands).

3) Know the date of your last vaccination, innoculation, place of birth and are honest about the sanity, or otherwise, of your parents.

Pretty grim!

Yours affectionately, Dick

QUIS Separabit

OR

" THE FREEDOM OF THE SEAS. "

Temple — with Knobs on.

My dear Walter,

Burma is definately the land of the PAGODA.

This is not a fruit, or climatic phenomina, but just an ordinary temple with Knobs on.

With regard to the people, two physical features are of outstanding importance, NECKS and CHINS.

As in Europe, the women have most of the neck, only in Burma they wrap strings of beads round it.

The Burmese seem to be elivided into tribes according to their chins

There are the Chins, Kachins, Knochins and Tuchins (or double chins).

NECK.

CHINS.

This unfair distribution of chins may in time lead to socialistic activities among the Knochins and the old Burmese policy, "an eye for an eye and a chin for a Chin" is likely to be inforced against the Tuchins under the slogan "Two chins for the rich and none for the poor".

Even so, the loyal toast of "chin chin" will always be drunk where ever Burmese forgather.

Yours affectionately,

Dick.

WELCOME TO BURMA.

My dear Walter,

Back to INDIA and the grindstone once more.

The grindstone, by the way, is not for my sword, but for my old razor blades.

Back to the grindstone.

I have still three weeks leave in hand and over one thousand miles to go before I complete my circumnavigation of the world. at DELHI.

CALCUTTA is the biggest port and city, in INDIA and does not like getting mixed up with provincial places like BOMBAY.

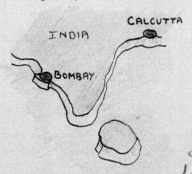

BOMBAY also stands on its dignity and does everything different to the way it is done in CALCUTTA.

Standing on dignity

In the past, high minded people have tried to bring these places together, but false pride and a couple of thousand miles of INDIA still keeps them apart.

Yours affectionately,

Dick

Still apart!

BACK TO THE GRINDSTONE.

BENARES.

25th November 1937.

My dear Walter,

This is BENARES, the great bathing place of INDIA on the banks of the GANGES.

HINDUS claim that the Ganges water at Benares is one hundred percent pure despite the thousands of bodies (dead and alive) and miles of drainage, that enter it daily. This claim has the support of learned medical men, but, even so, I would rather risk the DAK BUNGALOW Sodapāni — with a dash of something in it, of course.

Another purity campaign.

Ganges water 100% Pure

Dak Bungalow Soda pani & dash Pure? DANGER!

Limited mixed bathing is permitted at BENARES, although some of the gents bathing (or swim) suits are on the border line. Many others, however, are almost 'old fashioned' in their respectability.

Swim Suits.

What with cows, bicycles and temples, the bell noise is deafning. Thank goodness Hindus eat chapatties and not MUFFINS.

Yours affectionately,

Dick

HELLS BELLS.

GANGES LIDO

BENARES. THE GREAT INDIAN BATHING PLACE.

LUCKNOW.

4th December 1937.

My dear Walter,

LUCKNOW is steeped in

the memory of the successful defence
of the Residency during the Mutiny.

No doubt your history book
contains a picture of Flora Macdonald,

— so's christmas!

or Jenny Wren, exposing herself recklessly to the
enemy's fire and saying, "the Camels are comming"!

She had been roused to a frenzy (possibly from
a peaceful sleep) by the sound of the bagpipes.

"The Brain Fever Bird" does the same for
us during the hot weather.

GRAND TRUNK ROAD

From LUCKNOW I shall travel on the Grand
Trunk Road to Cawnpore and DELHI.

This is the way by which

the LUCKNOW RELIEF FORCE marched from Delhi, but

I hope I do not kill as many people on the road as
they did, otherwise I shall probably finish up without
a driving licence.

Times ar'nt what they were.

Yours affectionately,

Goodness! what's this one made of ?

THE FLAG STILL FLIES.

LUCKNOW.

DELHI.
7ᵗʰ DECEMBER 1937.

My dear Walter,

Today I reached DELHI and completed my circumnavigation of the globe from EAST to WEST (and back to EAST again). This is the same direction as Drake and all the best people sail.

DELHI is divided into two parts, New and OLD DELHI.

NEW DELHI is the cool weather home of the Viceroy and Government of INDIA.

OLD DELHI is the commercial part and was famous during the Mutiny of '57 as the place where a

All the BEST PEOPLE.

handfull of PUKKHA SAHIBS held the FORT by sitting on a ridge outside it in the middle of the hot weather instead of going up to Simla.

This, combined with the carelessness of some SAPPERS who first blew up the magazine and then the KASHMIR GATE, so enraged the enemy that they became sulky and refused to mutiny properly.

CONFOUND THOSE SAPPERS!

Tomorrow I shall continue my journey to LANDI KOTAL, but, from now onwards, instead of the compass I follow the drum.

Yours affectionately,

IMPERIAL DELHI.

WE ARE IN CHINA

OFF THE RECORD

" OFF THE RECORD "

Unofficial illustrations from the adventures

of

1ˢᵗ Bn. 5ᵗʰ Royal Gurkha Rifles. F.F.

in

World War Nº 2.

by

PORTLAND.

This stone was erected by men of the 1/5th Gurkhas on Miranjani, a 9800-foot peak some 25 miles from the old 5th Gurkhas regimental depôt at Abbottabad and one of Portland's favourite haunts.

The amateurish execution of the inscription touchingly underlines the mens' determination that this memorial should be the work of their own hands – work in which no outsider could have taken part.

PORTLAND
An Appreciation by
Colonel P. B. Winstanley MC

R. W. Morland-Hughes joined the 5th Royal Gurkha Rifles (Frontier Force) in September 1932 at Abbottabad in the North West Frontier Province. He was soon on active service with the 1st Battalion in 1933 at Bajaur in Mohmand territory and, in 1935, in the Black Mountains of Hazara. After his furlough in 1937 – covered irreverently in his letters herein to his brother Walter – he took part in the Waziristan campaign of 1938-9. So he soon got into that active working relationship with officers and Gurkhas which was the foundation of a comradeship in arms and pride of regiment that was special to the 5th Gurkhas and which he was always at pains to maintain.

His nickname, conjured by brother officers in the mess, was Portland Bill; the Bill was soon dropped. Amongst the Gurkhas a similarly friendly fraternity existed and they, too, gave him a name of their own which arose from an incident typical of Portland's character which so endeared him to the men. On manoeuvres, while his recruit company was crossing a railway line, a train approached. To young Gurkhas fresh from the Himalaya the sight and sound of a steam engine was awesome and it was with amazement and admiration that they saw Portland stride on to the track and stand, hand raised, fearlessly commanding the clanking, hissing monster to stop – which it did, belching smoke. The Gurkhas knew him as *railgari* (railway engine) from then on with respect, affection and amusement.

I joined the Regiment five years his junior and he soon became to me the model of an officer and leader I aspired to emulate. We shared many an expedition with our Gurkhas into the foothills of the Kashmiri ranges. Miranjani mountain he specially liked. After the war the Gurkha Major built a stone memorial to Portland which stands on the summit. It is a fitting tribute to the man and to that understanding of loyalty and regimental honour which cemented the special relationship he had with the steadfast Gurkhas. One of his Commanding Officers wrote of him: 'You can have no idea what an influence for good he was and how the success of the Battalion was due to his efforts in no small way! he was fonder of the men than anyone, yet he was never soft with them and always maintained strict discipline.' That his men would follow him anywhere would become evident in the war which was to come.

Having served as Quartermaster and Training Company Commander, Portland was Adjutant when the Battalion left for the Middle East in June 1941, where it was to help stabilise the situation in Iraq, Persia and Syria. As Adjutant it was one of his tasks to write up the daily war diary. 'Off the Record' portrays events of this rather unglamorous period with perception and humour. For the performance of his official duties he was awarded the MBE.

In September 1943 the Battalion, with Portland now second-in-command, moved to Italy with the 8th Indian Division and began the drive northwards against German resistance and impeded by a series of rivers flowing across the line of advance. In the course of these actions the Commanding Officer was wounded and Portland assumed command of the Battalion on 10 November 1943. His immediate task was to attack the enemy in Atessa, a village strongly held by first-class German troops and commanding the approach to the Sangro which formed the outer edge of the heavily defended Gustav line. There was insufficient cover for an attack by day, but night patrols established the location of the Germans' forward defences, and the assault, led by Portland in person, was launched on the night of 12 November. The outer defences were overrun, the counter-attack by the main body in Atessa was repulsed after fierce fighting and the enemy finally routed at a cost to us of only sixteen wounded. Throughout the action Portland's complete disregard for his own safety, though suffering a facial wound, had inspired his men by whom there were many acts of valour. His roused spirit with the Gurkhas he led rejoicing in their victory gave the inspiration to illuminate for higher authority the importance of his action. It fell to me to write the citation for the immediate award to Portland of a Military Cross for his personal courage and leadership. It was not until I revisited the scene of the battle twelve years later that I fully appreciated the vital tactical importance of the German position which Portland's astute military mind had grasped at once.

The advance northwards continued with further heavy fighting. On 17 June 1944, with Portland once again in command, the Battalion reached Ripa ridge, the outer bastion of a naturally strong defensive position. By 19 June the ridge had been taken. Portland, keen to press on, went forward to reconnoitre. On his way back he was mortally wounded by shellfire but refused to be evacuated until he had handed over in detail the results of his reconnaissance and his orders for a further advance. He died before the dressing station could be reached. Portland died as he would have wished, in command of the Battalion, leading the men he loved and served with such honour and fulfilling to the highest degree that military duty to which he had dedicated his life.

This was the Happy Warrior
This was He!

The 1st BN declares war on Germany
3 Sep 39

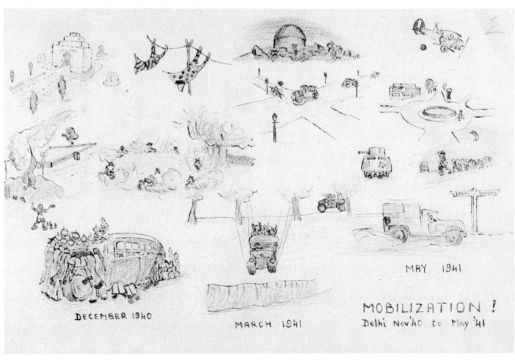

DECEMBER 1940

MARCH 1941

MAY 1941

MOBILIZATION !
Delhi Nov'40 to May '41

49

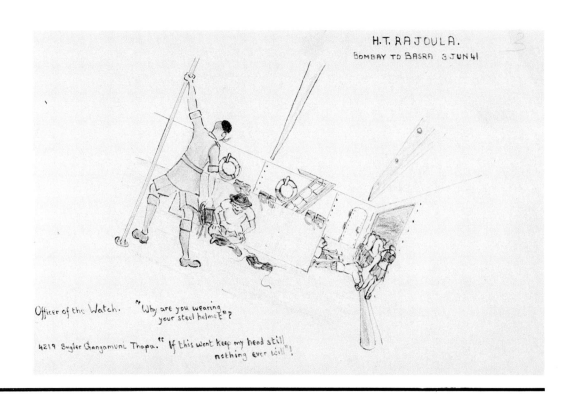

Officer of the Watch.   "Why are you wearing your steel helmet"?

4219 Bugler Gangamuni Thapa. "If this wont keep my head still nothing ever will"!

OPPOSED LANDING.   BASRA 9 JUN 41.

COCKYOLLY BIRD. "I did'nt get time to collect any orders for you. They wont help you in any case. No one here knows when you will disembark, or where you should go to if you do • If you require my assistance you will not be able to find me as I shall be resting in my day cabin."

BASRA JULY 1941

MOVEMENT CONTROL. ARRANGE THE DISEMBARCATION OF SERIAL Nº 47.
1/5 A.G.R. will provide guides, conducting party, tpt etc.

FRIENDS, GUIDES AND HOSTS!
Mr DIX and Staff of the KHANAQIN OIL Refinery
KHANAQIN August 1941.

"CRACK TROOPS"
D 16 qualifies.
MOSUL   JANUARY 1942.

"DIGGING UP THE PAST"

Making the 1917 Turkish position at AL FATHA GORGE face the other way
AL FATHA   APRIL 1942.

"WAR SHIPS OF THE DESERT"
OR
"JOCK COLS"

AL FATHA   MAY 1942.

"WARM RECEPTION"
HABBYANIA JUNE 1942
·at 130° shade.

Officer. What is it ? —Heatstroke ?
Signaller No —the Colonel Sahib !

"From one Theatre of Operations to Another"!
IRAQ TO SYRIA JULY 1942.

"CIVILIZATION AT LAST"!
OR
"The C.O. and the Cistern"
ALEPPO JULY 1942.

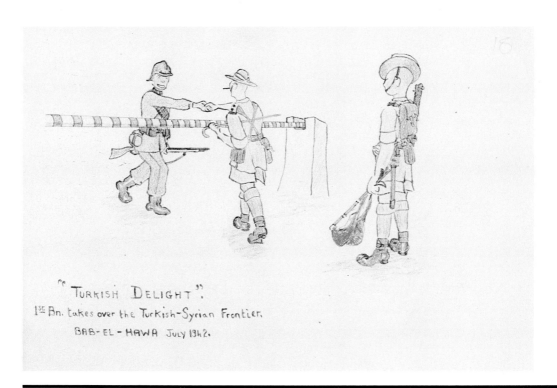

"TURKISH DELIGHT".
1st Bn. takes over the Turkish-Syrian Frontier.
BAB-EL-HAWA July 1942.

"ON THE ROCKS"
LATTAQUIE OCTOBER 1942.

Jumbo said to Paiforce,
"I love you"!

Paiforce said to Jumbo,
"We don't believe you do"!

"'Cause if you really loved us,
Like you say you do,"

"You wouldn't go to Cairo,
and leave us under Q". !

Paiforce.
Feb 1943.

KIFRI
SUPPLEMENT.
MARCH TO APRIL 1943.

BALING OUT
IN THE DESERT
(BAGHDAD TO DAMASCUS)
APRIL 1943.

TROUBLE IN THE CAMP.
(BAALBEK)
MAY 1943.

Conspiracy.

Mutiny

Open Revolt.

CAPTIONS

Page 49, top: There is a gentle irony here, for the Battalion had recently returned from the Waziristan operations of 1938-9 and were now peacefully in cantonments at Abbottabad. Many of them felt that the second German War might pass them by. In the event some officers were soon called, as mountain warfare experts, to take part in the Norway campaign of 1940. **Bottom:** The transition from mule to motor transport started on old bazaar buses and bicycles and graduated to army trucks and motorcycles. Manoeuvres included reconnaissance, route marches, night driving across country without lights and using tanks (powered by Gurkhas' feet). A veritable pyre of Molotov cocktails added to the fun.

Page 50, top: Gurkhas were unaccustomed to sea voyages. They had even, indeed, to perform a costly religious cleansing ceremony when returning to Nepal from across the 'black waters' – remedies for sea sickness had no place in their lore. **Bottom:** The Battalion's arrival at Basra in Iraq, in a temperature of 110°F with 98 per cent humidity, was not allowed to ruffle the dignified and, in their view, disgraceful calm of the Movement Control Officer who became known, in consequence, as the Cocky Olly Bird. Living up to the motto of that sublime branch of the Staff, ('All control and no movement OR, all movement and no control') he left it to the Gurkhas to unload the entire regimental transport, stores and ammunition. They accomplished all with a few rickety dockside cranes before dawn broke, the first night of their arrival.

Page 51, top: The Cocky Olly Bird having done less than well on their arrival was determined to do better for the arrival of the Battalion's first re-inforcement. The draft had a large serial number but consisted of one man. **Bottom:** By August 1941 Persia, as Iran was still called, was full of German 'tourists' and Russian fifth columnists who were planning between them to take over and divide the country. The Battalion was camped at Khanaqin beside the Anglo-Persian oil refinery just inside Iraq. The manager, Mr Dix, accompanied officers disguised, in borrowed clothes, as oil prospectors to points of view which he well knew. The invasion, under General Slim, took place on 25 August and after the surrender of the Persian Army the Battalion reached Teheran on 18 September where they met the Russians as Allies.

Page 52, top: An unprecedented spell of arctic weather with thirty degrees of frost at night suddenly struck at Mosul. Major Peter Fordham suggested that, to avoid cylinder blocks from cracking, the engines might be kept warm by various means. He made a great sacrifice by offering his hot water bottle. All were astounded that he should have so essentially female an item of equipment. **Bottom:** This old Turkish position was still littered with Ottoman equipment, perfectly preserved in the dry sand a few inches under the surface. The sand was smelly, full of vipers and had even grown a cornfield, a few inches across, from grains spilt in 1917 from Turkish mule troughs. *Dudhdanra,* Gurkhali for a milky hill, was often a feature of military landscapes described for the purpose of fire orders.

Page 53, top: Western desert-type naval formation tactics proved impracticable in Iraq temperatures of 160°F in the sun. Touching the armour of a Bren carrier meant an instant blister. Nor was a ration of one water bottle per man per day sensible. The artist, always a disciplinarian, himself refrained from water until, at 10am, he had heatstroke and was ordered by the CO to drink. **Bottom:** Newly issued No 18 wireless sets made communication with Battalion HQ much more frequent – and intimate. For *Habbyania* read *Habbaniya.*

Page 54, top: Matron is a caricature of General 'Jumbo' Wilson, C-in-C Middle East Command. **Bottom:** After fifteen months in desert country the Battalion arrived in Aleppo to relieve the Australians. They were housed, at first, in French colonial barracks which seemed to promise comfort. But it was hardly so. Not only had the vandals stolen lead piping from such vital areas as the CO's specially selected convenience, but the place was lice-ridden. The Battalion soon moved out to the more accustomed, if airy, cleanliness of tents outside the town.

Page 55, top: Tommy Marsden, commanding B Company, was the first to make friendly contact at the Gate of the Wind with the Turkish Army border guards. Having been on the losing side in the last war the Turks were taking no chances this time. **Bottom:** Peter Fordham, with D Company, meanwhile was disporting on the Mediterranean shore at Lattakia, still under command of a rather bombastic old French General called Montcalm. Even so, local Syrian arabs were not prevented from sniping the town and so relaxation was still under guard.

Page 57, top: General 'Jumbo' Wilson left Paiforce to take over command of the Middle East and Forces and General Quinan took over. The Battalion had served under the latter in Waziristan 1938-9.

Page 58, top: Apart from unseasonable rain the journey resulted in sixteen casualties thrown out of trucks through Indian drivers falling asleep on the desert roads. **Bottom:** The Battalion camped in sight of Roman ruins at Baalbek. Old British Nissen huts were billets and the mutiny depicted was minor for Itwari, the head sweeper, found himself, due to water-borne sewage, out of work except for sweeping the dust. The mess cats almost immobilised the outfit by blocking the drains. Preparatory to the invasion of Italy roundels were being newly painted on all vehicle bonnets. One of the despatch riders decided to make himself immune from the RAF.